WALKING IN THE GARDEN OF WORDS

Victor Fein

DEDICATION:

I am grateful to those along the way who inspired and encouraged me to express myself through the written word. Thanks to my brother Vern, my wife Bobbie, and my son Forest as well as the wonderful poetry group I have attended for years—The Champaign- Urbana Poetry Group.

CONTENTS

AT THIS MOMENT

At this moment
this very moment
Somewhere a child cries
An alarm sounds

She feels the pain
of the first time
Laughter penetrates the air
A kettle whistles its ready

The last strain introduces a new life
While A car crash takes a life
Lips touch
A home run is hit

At this moment
She slides her foot into her high-heeled shoe
Dirt is shoveled on a casket
A shot is fired killing a black man

A rose begins to unfold
While he says " I do"
A lion takes down a gazelle
A fish is caught for wanting a minnow

Three brothers embrace
Happy Father's day is spoken
While somewhere a helicopter is shot down.

At this very moment
Birds build a nest
While a cat waits for its time

Rains flood while drought cracks the earth
A poet finds a line to express her feelings

This moment
This very moment
The moon waits its turn to be full
Women dance to drum beats
While the ocean swallows a ship

Joy swells hearts
While sorrow shrinks them

Nails are pounded through His hands
While he wonders where his Father is

The sun rises for some
While it sets for others
A seedling breaks earth's surface
While a tree falls

Life Expressing itself
In these moments

PASSAGES

I look at him
gently swinging in
a hammock
across the room
his coal black unruly hair
large sculpted body
unusually handsome
man face
my mind drifts back
he is a child sitting on my lap
I feel his warmth
his weight
his love
my legs now numb
circulation hindered
he has become too large
to sit on my lap any longer
I don't want to say it
have resisted putting words to it
for some time
each word tumbles

from my lips
like a slow motion landslide
Son
you
are
too
big
now
to
sit
on

my
lap
It hurts to say it
It hurts not to say it.

MORNING

My eyes open slowly
greeted by the rising sun's orange glow.
The ocean waves, a bird's call,
the sound of a falling coconut,
the pouring of coffee splashing in my cup
tickle my ears.
Half awake, half asleep
I make my way to the patio.
The early sun now sparkles, dances on the ocean surface.
Above me a tree sheds tiny blossoms some falling in my coffee
cup,
while others scatter about like golden snowflakes.
Yet another tree encouraged by a passing breeze sheds tiny
orange berries never to turn to fruit
Back home a new president takes office today.
I consciously put aside my homeland's misfortune for now in this
special
space knowing upon my return I will be dunked
in the polluted waters of our new reality.

A WAY OUT

I need something to divert my mind
It keeps being drawn to dark spaces where fear sits around
on chairs and couches, patting the seat next to them
beckoning me to join them
part of me knows better
part of me is drawn to them
I feel my psyche moving toward the couch
I hesitate then reach for a pill
opening the bottle
I pause ask myself
is there another way
to stay out of this psychic cave
I need to focus on my breathing
breathe deeply slowly
cast out the slithering angst
inhabiting my being
suddenly I feel a presence
I look side to side
then behind me but see no one
I can feel it though
a feeling like when you know
you are being looked at
I go within in search of this presence
the spirit of light and love
appears in human form
It reaches its hand out for me to grasp
I notice a deep scar on His palm
our hands unite
we walk together
out of the darkness

IN MY DAY

summer meant
running through the neighborhood
with friends
playing marbles
kick the can
hide n seek
mom yelled dinner
then outside again
till the street lights glowed
winter took us inside
I lucky enough
to have a brother
made up games
baseball cards
on the bedroom floor
basketball
a rolled up sock
thrown thru the curtain rod
Monopoly
ping pong
Clue
many seasons
have come and gone
since those days
my brother and I
still hang out
age has altered our games
now we fish
and talk about
our children's' children's play
though they don't play
in the neighborhood
don't play marbles

don't play
hide n seek
nor kick the can
they play games
on screens
hardly ever look up
makes you wonder

what their children
will do for play

EVOLUTION

it is quite interesting
living in this physical form
the one mom and dad
put together in their pleasure
It came with parts of her
parts of him
parts of ancestors
whose face and form
I will not ever know
this nose
this cleft in my chin
passed on from father
given to him by someone
in the past
the thick hair
the sagging under
my eyes
who passed that to me
was it great aunt Sally
uncle Sam
or great grandpa Morrie
was intellectual ability
included in this hand me down
process
did somewhere along
my lineage
perhaps a religious leader
lead his people
to the promised land
was there a
warrior
who slaughtered
for the of want

of power
it all leaves me
turning the pages
of history
wondering
in the future
what will be expressed
by my son's
son or daughter
might they have
my eyes
perhaps be an engineer
an artist
or a poet

could they
find an answer
to cancer
or turn around
the environmental
crisis
through them I live on

BURIED ALIVE

deep in the redwood forest
attending a mens' retreat
standing before
a hundred men
he looks down
his voice quivers
been eating off the bottom
like a catfish
sucking in any fuckin' thing I can
to make it through another day
trapped in the hood
feels like a barrel of crabs
trying to scratch
their way out of a bucket
know what I'm sayin
mamas an alcoholic
sis she was raped
by my Grandfather
committed suicide
know what I sayin'
silence
thick as mud
my brother's
he's a gang bangin'
doin' crack
sellin' drugs
I can't feel nothin'
so I cut myself

HOMECOMING

one day
she slipped away
like the sun moving behind a cloud
there yet no longer in view
herself

her personality
hiding inside fear's purse
where are you
lift the latch
open the hatch
Slip from the grip
of this cruel freak
chemicals changed
rearranged
Your still there
so come back
to the one you are meant to be
after a long period of agony
peer from the dungeon
the bars that enclose you
begin to bend
openings appear
beckoning come out
come out
rip away the straps
that confine you
open the jar
let them free
let the fireflies
light your way
there you are
I see you

come take my hand
the journey is near end
let us dance to new life
to resurrection
welcome home my love
I have missed you….

GRACE

a magnificent
shimmering white
swan
golden beak
crowned in ebony
out of water
it waddles
body swaying
side to side
lacking coordination
lacking grace
in the water
its element
a startling beauty
of elegance
one has to wonder
where we waddle
where is our
element
is there a place where
we flow
where our soul
slips into the water
to make us
kings or queens
of elegance
where
our full potential
Glows

WATERSHED

The bright, early afternoon sun pierced through a maze of
leaves,
glistening the black feathers of a large crow resting on a
pine branch.

Below, two hikers sit across from one another at a picnic table
preparing for their journey.

The crow's yellow encircled black, beady eyes focus upon them,
reflecting their image
while it complains repeatedly with raspy caws echoing through
the gorge.

The picnic table's bold, thick structure securely holds the two
men.
One entering his middle age, the other his old age—father and son
in transition.

The graying table top displays the artwork of many apprentice
carvers.
Butterflies, hearts encircling initials of lovers, crude faces and
random symbols.

Off to one end of the table sits a glass jar, lid securely fastened.
Its uneven surface reflects light in many directions.
Floating to the top mushroom caps seem to want to escape while
their stems lie peacefully on the bottom.

The liquid within the color of golden honey indicates its
readiness.
Walking slowly and quietly to one side a long-legged blue heron
wades through the stream hunting for lunch
its sharp beak poised in readiness grasps an unsuspecting fish.

Dedication, intention, silence prevail in preparation for ingestion
of the tea.
Will the spores invoke insight, offer wisdom?

The liquid quenching their thirst
while opening the door to the anticipated journey.

The placid lake reflects blue skies and shadows of ancestral,
huge pine trees offering a beautiful canvas to rest their eyes upon
as the tea begins to affect their state of presence.

Conversation fills the near silence, camouflaging the soft whisper
of the breeze through the pine needles.
Hearts embrace.

Presence, this is about presence.
Dropping into the moment.

They recognize this place they have visited before.
This place where time slows.
This place where the moment is right in front of you.

This place where clarity brings to focus the reminder of the
contrast of then and now.
Thoughts floating in the moment, no longer bothered by the
intrusion of past or future unless deliberately unearthed to reveal
within.

Hours pass in this timeless state, not being noticed as time…….
only now.
Father and son sharing life together while they have it.

Sharing time as the spores influence begins to diminish,
holding fast the love and connection once more from this land of
clarity and presence.

RETURN THE GOODS

there has been a burglary
age has tampered
with the locks
broken into my body
taken parts
damaged others
generally defiled
my systems
there has been a burglary
energy that allowed me
whatever I needed
diminished
ripped off stolen
there has been a burglary
the thief has
taken hair
dimmed sight
hearing
taken strength
diminished desire
where are the
age police
arrest this culprit
get back my belongings
return to me
the gifts of youth

VALUABLES

There are those that would come to rob me
take what

they see as valuable
jewels, money, electronics

not knowing my valuables
are not those

they cannot take my
memories
thoughts
loving relationships

deep in the closet of my being
I place treasured thoughts
only to be opened by those
with a key to my heart

A WALK IN THE HOOD

walking in my neighborhood
a warm late summer day

observing the sidewalk cracks
I remember as a youth saying
step on a crack and break
Hitler's back

in the distance
a man heads my way
seems tall
on the thin side
too far to know for sure

his vibe feels friendly
his gait seems firm
yet soft

a squirrel rushes madly
across my intended path
I wondered why he is so afraid
is it my size
did his mother warn him
is it in his genetic code

a lovely garden appears
bees seem delighted
to have the beautiful blossoms
submissively open to their desires

a motorcycle
no muffler
roars past

disturbing the peace
no wonder squirrels run

the once distant man draws closer
I wonder if he will acknowledge
my presence

many I pass
on my daily walks
don't look at me
they have sound buds in their ears
a glassy look in their eyes
zombie-like

others an I Phone in hand
so focused on it
I am invisible

women passing
some seem afraid
to make contact
even a glance

the tall thin man arrives
I look in his eyes
as we approach
I nod my head
a mild smile
he returns it

it feels good to
share a moment with
a stranger
to be seen

TWELVE YEARS A FRIEND

never knew
what gender
to give you

he
she
them
they

looked under
the hood
nothing there
to help

we have been
through many
miles together

one hundred
forty thousand
of them

twelve years
of adventure
of arrivals
of departures

high speed travel
wind whipping
your sides

insect
bodies slamming

your windows
and hood

slow cruise
gazing
taking in
the beauty
around us

through rain
through snow
heat and cold

heated leather seats
you always
keep me warm

hot air circulating
on those
blustery cold days

comfortable on
scorching summer days
cool air blowing
through my hair

the time
that tire blew
you swerved violently

yet kept
me safe
out of harms way

you have
been a partner
in movement
serving me well

we have grown
older together
our senses
diminished

the new car
equipped with modern
technology to aid
aging drivers

Motivates me
to move on

time now
to part ways
my old silver friend

as I hand
over the keys
emotion rises

be safe
take good care
of these folks

like you did
my family
and me

roll on
my friend
roll on

TRAPPED

sitting in a room with over a hundred men
sharing life stories
to release
to feel compassion
Empathize

words burrow deep in our souls
we weep together
laugh together

this man's sister
and mother committed suicide
while he was out in the hood selling
to keep the family in food

this man killed three people
knifed them to death
stood over them
watched them bleed out
one by one

twenty seven years in prison
sleeping with his actions
out now two years
he works to help boys
find heathy direction

recently being informed
he is not potent
never to have a son
he has dreamed of
stands before us
screaming

weeping his loss

this young man
eighteen
stands
pauses
takes several deep breaths
tells us he has no chance
his words crumble
like broken glass

no direction
little education
I'm white
don't make no difference man
I have no one

foster parents
I hate them
never knew my father
ma is dead
sister she overdosed
got nothin man

another can hardly express
the trauma of that day
he shot and killed
who they told him
was the enemy

pain
guilt
fear
dripping from their tongues
saturating our hearts

brotherhood
pulls us together
units us
hugs us
soothes us

A BAD HAND

years of defeat in Vietnam

should have enlightened our leaders

to fold knowing they had a poor hand,

they didn't,

a poker game war

no one was bluffing,

Instead they raised the stakes betting our young

betting our kids like poker chips in the pot,

infiltrating their brains through patriotism.

It took years to finally step away from the table.

GOOD OLE DAYS

Remember those days
when your skin was tight

when your eyes were bright
and offered good sight

When hearing was keen
like a well-oiled machine

sense of smell
precise as well

your legs carried your frame
with little of no pain

those days were the best
I invite them to return as my guest

SPECIAL DAY

today is a special day
you might ask why

it is special
because
birds
are singing

the sun is
nourishing
life

early morning
rain gives drink

leaves dance
in the gentle breeze

because flowers
splash vivid colors
like fallen confetti
across the landscape

bees and
dragon flies
glide through
blue skies

because a drone
dropped off a
love letter
from my
wife

because
I awoke
this morning
to a lovely tune
playing in my mind

because I woke up
this morning

it is a special day

PEACE BY THE SEA

Hanging out in a small
sea side village
in Central America

things move slowly here
seems no reason
not to

peace and
cooperation
come easily

saw a cat lying
next to a mouse
legs in the air

thought it dead
till the cat's tail twitched
brushed against it

the mouse causally
looked over
at the cat
and yawned

ocean waves unfold
leisurely here
hardly

a sound
less they wake
a napper

pelicans cruise
the wind
in formation
wings straight out
soaring in
slow motion
not a care in the world

siesta lasts hours
leaving little time
for work

not much to do
no need to do it
in a hurry
leaving
nothing to do

ever hear
a hummingbird
snore
they do here

iguana basking
in the sun
half chewed
leaf hanging
from it's mouth

monkeys
hang out
lazily groom
each other
eating what
they find

special this
little village
by the sea

THE STICK POEM

an unexpected
phone call

the words
tumble from the ear piece
like a landslide
of boulders
crushing my heart

she is dead
echoes over and over
she is dead
she is dead

falling to my knees
waterfall tears
soak my thoughts

a day later
walking the beach
shared stories of her
with my wife and son

I'm drawn to waters edge
a small stick
beckons my attention

a voice whispers
louder than the ocean waves
pick it up
my hand obeys

there before me
a sun-bleached stick
blue ink letters
the words hand-written

"There is no greater love
than a mother's love for her
child. "

I gasp
chills saturate my being
my heart pounds
breath abandons

a moment in time
two realms
embrace

MONARCH

sitting in the yard
soothed by sound of
falling water in the pond

attention is drawn
to a crimson cardinal
landing on the feeder

a moment later the flight
of a gorgeous Monarch
is observed
wings spread
floating on the morning breeze

a gentle flutter
here and there directs her
to a Dahlia bursting
with yellow splendor

a zinnia
a cone flower
all the colorful blooms
beckon her to land

petals spread wide
her probing
tickling their antlers
spreading pollen
plant to plant

she pauses on the milkweed
as if she has found home
grounded on it
her wings gently fan her

suddenly
as if frightened
by an enemy
the cardinal
Monarch soars
out of sight

leaving only the
sound of falling water

THE SOUND OF SILENCE

one dog barks
another barks
then another
echoing through
the neighborhood
dog dominoes

helicopter blades whirl
wind whips
noise each turn

takes a special muffler
or no muffler at all
to produce a roar
so disturbing the impulse is
to cover your ears

neighborhood woodworkers
saws and sander sounds
blanket bird songs

blowers and mowers screech
and rumble
as high pitch sounds abound

A siren
the grinding of a downed tree
a train rumbles past
noise, noise
everywhere

leaving little room
where a bird may be heard

the rustle of leaves
in the breeze

moments of
the sound of silence
are blaring quiet.

FATHER AND SON

perched on a veranda
second story of a small hotel

my view offers
witness

to a boy playing
games with his father

running after one another
laughing

flinging a frisbee
diving for the catch

enjoying the moment
while the boy is still a boy
before time grows
him to a man

when the games
will no longer be as they are
at this moment

game over
they hug briefly

line up for racing
side by side race posture

father wins this one
while he can

LIFE AS A DESSERT

Think about it
what is your
very favorite
dessert?

imagine it on
a magnificent
plate
before you

each bite
diminishes
it's size

like
your life
diminishes
each passing day

bite
by
bite

the size
grows smaller
life grows
shorter

suddenly
about to
cut off a piece

awareness

becomes
focussed
on the size

bites deliberately
become smaller
attempting to
lengthen
what remains

appreciation
accelerates
expands

conscious
awareness
explodes

with each
remaining
bite

as each
remaining
day

becomes
more precious

L..O..V ..E..

born with the capacity
to love

capable of empathy
of compassion

we enter this earth
the same way

with a mother
to receive us

a breast
to feed us

umbilical chord
cut to release us

the journey begins

some mothers
turn away
not ready

some fathers
reject deny
walk away

(how) can this infant
know love
know how to feel it
how to give it
if no model

yet within
Its being
the seed is there
waiting to blossom

watered by kindness
warmed by
a smile

nurtured by an
outreached
hand
a love song

even lacking
a teacher
the seed of love

can grow
rooted in the heart

AMAZON IN THE AMAZON

slogging through the dense jungle

deep in the Amazon

I arrive in at Shipibo healing center
there before me a shaman

swaying in a hammock

I Phone in hand

my heart contracts

breath pauses

at the sight

oh no

I want to scream

this tribe has been corrupted

corporate America has slithered

through the jungle

like an Anaconda

infecting as it goes

pure culture thinned

corporate bottom line profit motive

is eating the planet

sucking the liquid oil from its veins

cutting and grinding its trees

polluting its air

defiling its water

corroding cultures

it is to late

the seeds are planted

and growing

the indigenous
have been contaminated

BIG SAM

Sam was twelve
Sam was big
bigger than all the other players
in our Little League division

His size 12 shoes
six foot two inches tall frame
made for a legendary pitcher
known also for his lack of control.

Everyone was intimidated
to face Sam at the plate.
I was knocked silly when he hit my helmet
and painfully experienced a second "take your base"
when hit on the fingers holding my bat.

I was chosen at eleven years old to catch for Sam
during the end of the year
Little league tournament in the region
I was little, little enough to be able to stand, consciously bracing
myself while receiving many of Sam's fast balls.

I was relieved to not have to bat against Sam.
We played well together winning our regional
tournament.

ALLURING

opening my old tackle box
my mind rewinds
like reeling in my fishing line

that morning
soon after sunrise
the rope pulled
a puff of smoke
the outboard motor gurgles
as we float from the shore line

unique time
wc young boys and
our father

morning mist floats
just above the water
birds swoop and dive
distant loon calls
echo across the lake

anchored down
poles in hand
excitement builds
load your hook

minnows squirm
as the hook slips
through their tiny bodies

we are told silence is good
noise scares the fish away
the wake of another boat
rocks us enough we grip our seats

bobbers bob
eyes glued on them
waiting for a sign
suddenly it submerges
my pole bends

instructions begin
"Let him run with it,
okay now reel in some,
easy don't rush it,
Get the net."

nice one hold tight
so it won't fin you
pull the hook out
get the stringer

the days' catch is good
hold them up for a photo
who got the biggest
who got the most

A day on the water
just the guys

recalling those precious moments
I close the old tackle box

say to my boy
come on son
let's go fishin'

NOT ENOUGH

born with endless potential
anything imaginable
perceived
possible
somewhere along the way
a seed was planted
a seed of doubt
germinating self criticism
along the way
it received the nourishment
it needed to flourish
re-enforced
it settles in
infiltrates
roots spread
enveloping
the mind
like kudzu
all that potential
tangled
enmeshed
in feelings of not enough
not worthy
years of struggle
seeking to find
confidence
find one's self
determined to
destroy the monster
that stole
his soul
rustle
through the piles

of files in one's
mental attic
dust off
memories
search
through history
then one day
light shined
through the muck
there in the distance
waving
stood hope
affirmation
clarity
freedom lies on
the other side of
awareness

THE CATCH

Crouched like a Cheetah
anticipating the attack,
eyes focused on the batter.
Final inning ,
leading by one run,
opposing team on first and third,
two outs.
Win this game
guaranteed fourth place
in this National softball tournament.
Batter poised
two strikes,
two balls.
pitcher releases
It is hit hard.
A low flying line drive
assisted by the wind.
Running faster than I thought capable
I view the ball rapidly descending.
Off season my mitt a ball placed within
is rubber- banded to create a pocket.
A pocket this ball might find a home in.
I lunge forward
leaving my feet
momentarily in flight,
arm fully extended.
The ball hits the glove hard
almost ripping it from my grip.
I hit the ground rolling
ball embedded deep within
that pocket so defined.
Momentarily disoriented,
heart pounding

I gather myself
stand with glove and ball extended high
to testify the catch, the conquest.
The cheering, standing crowd
is thrilled by my catch.
Some sit stunned, disappointed.
My teammates smother me.
While waiting for the next game
I recall polio robbing me
fifty seven years ago
of half the Little league season.
Unable to run.
Weeks in the hospital,
the daily painful therapy.
Now at sixty seven being known
for my speed.
The newspaper referred to me as " Young Wheels."

REVOLUTION

We rode the same YELLOW SUBMARINE
consciously traveled the same waters
meeting in psychedelic STRAWBERRY FIELDS
dancing to the drumbeat of our time
While on a MAGICAL MYSTERY TOUR
SARGENT PEPPER led the march
chanting
GIVE PEACE A CHANCE
DO YOU WANT TO KNOW A SECRET
WITH A LITTLE HELP FROM MY FRIENDS
we knew we could open minds to explore
raising food awareness
environmental consciousness
women's rights
civil rights
Anti- war sentiment
we felt we could not LET IT BE
we believed we could
COME TOGETHER
and take down the FOOL ON THE HILL
It was a LONG AND WINDING ROAD
a HARD DAYS NIGHT
transforming separateness
replacing it with togetherness
believing ALL YOU NEED IS LOVE

PROSE:

OMENA TAMERAC

We met while visiting an art store far north in Michigan.
We had dropped our son off at a volleyball camp where he
would seek to improve his already unusual ability with the game.
My wife and I continued north stopping here and there to appre-
ciate the beauty of the state. Small towns we visited were often
charming and unique.
Our art store visit brought us face to face with Omena. She was
sitting on a bench made of natural tree branches. At the time of
our meeting, she was with two other aging women, apparently
gossiping . Omena sat with her left hand raised to her mouth and a
look on her face expressing embarrassment at what her friend was
sharing. She was wearing a tan cotton dress, an off white
crocheted sweater and brown shoes. Her white hair
and spectacles clarified her elderly status.
It only took a brief glance to surmise she and her friends might
have burned their bras back in the Sixties .
"Shall we consider asking her to come home with us? It would be
nice to have her in our family." We inquired and were assured she
could come with us. Our emotions were stirred as she was taken
from her two friends and slid into a large black plastic bag.
We placed her in the back of our Volvo station wagon for the
return trip.
Off we went on our way back to gather our son from camp.
He was all enthused by his experience, yet ready to go home. I
opened the back of the car to put his luggage
in when I was reminded of Omena cooped up in that
bag." Son, look, we have a new friend." I slid her from the black
bag expecting a positive response.
"I don't like her! She is spooky," he exclaimed, walking away to
gather his composure. He reacted as if we had a dead body we
were hiding.

"You will like her in time, son."
Omena has sat on one end of our couch for 32 years now. When
we leave for a vacation we sit her on a different couch. Someone
approaching our home will see the back of her through the front
window. We assume no one would break-in knowing
there was a sweet old lady sitting waiting for her two friends to
come and tell her the latest gossip.

BENEATH THE SURFACE

If you were to dig where the asteroid hit, through the crust then
the mantle.
Every three feet deep you dig, you go back in history ten thou-
sand years.
Layer by layer unfolding the story of Earth's history.

If I dig below the surface of my personal history
I discover a time, teased by patriotism, when I thought I was
doing good by joining the Army. I spied on the Vietnamese troop
movement then reported it to our command so they would know
where to attack and about how many of the enemy they would
likely encounter.

A mound of time since then I look back and realize patriotism
doesn't' excuse my contributing to the death of many people. War
is war, it kills solders as well as innocent people who have no
guns, have no weapons of any type. Families are torn apart
forever.

I want to shovel the layer of dirt back over the hole and hide that
history as I am sure many of us would love to do but it is too late.
It is there in those layers as part of our story. We have to wonder
who will unearth our time and be astounded by our behavior, by
the things we did to Mother Earth and her people.

ABANDON CAN

When a restaurant opened near campus and
begins to sell pizza by the slice, I thought I would try it out.
After receiving my slice of— sausage, onion and green pepper—
I made my way up stairs to the second floor.
Across the room the entire wall was made of glass.
Making my way, enticed by the sunlight's invitation,
I sat next to the window looking out toward campus.
A new convertible car pulled into the one un-occupied space just
below my view. A familiar man exited his car, paused, reached in
his pocket to to get the coins needed to feed the meter. Leaving
now he took a swig of his can of Pepsi, looked around to see if
anyone was watching before setting the can on the curb a few feet
from the back of the car in front of his.
He steps away, stops again to see if he had been seen by anyone.
Above his line of sight I watched the entire event. He, a local
lawyer, had the awareness to know he should not have abandon
his can on the curb. He walked away knowing the judge would
have found him guilty.

TIMELESS

Walking past a house on a dusty, bumpy road, in a hot foreign
Land intrigued monkeys watch from trees above.
a slow motion glance reveals a man and a woman
sitting on the porch of a rickety wood and tin house.
They greet me warmly shouting out an enthusiastic, "hola se-
nor!"
The man smiles his toothless smile and waves to me.
They seem excited to see someone, perhaps anyone.
They are many kilometers from any kind of town.
I wondered how they spend their days.
No antenna, no satellite dish, no sign of
technology anywhere in sight. No schedule for any event.
I imagined days going by spending time just
enjoying the rising and setting of the sun.
I think about my culture's need for recognition,
need to be famous,
to be known,
to be busy,
to climb the ladder.
I pause on the road to take in a more detailed look. Several
uninterested chickens peck
at the ground as if they are looking for meaning.
A colorful, proud rooster runs toward me with a hostile gait
warning me to keep my distance from his ladies.
The old man rises from his chair.
He slowly limps over to converse but my lack of Spanish greatly
limits our communication.
I note his bare feet hardened and oddly shaped.
I imagine he has not been wearing shoes for quite some time.
His skin over soaked in the sun, looks dry and leathery.
He seems interested in where I am going given there is nothing
Nearby but this dusty road lined by dense tropical forest.
I do not know how to explain that my

rented car broke down a kilometer or so up the road.
I try to explain but even with my hand dance, arms flailing, it
escapes his understanding. We smile, nod, as if we have commu-
nicated, I moved on.
A glance back allows a view of the old couple sitting on
their porch likely having experienced the excitement of the day
while the rooster continues guarding his ladies.

MIND GAMES

The Melatonin is hanging on each eye lid attempting to close
shop for the night.
My mind floats off like a kite torn from its restraints.
A figure comes visiting. Before me stands my own ego, intro-
duces itself, as if I did not recognize it.
"It has been quite a ride, I proclaim." It agrees than disappears
behind a thought.
My son and wife accompany me down an alleyway into a
mushroom shaped dream. There we are, the little family that
could and did. Each traveling alone for some time in search of
our souls. On occasion we check in with one another.
During those times we blend into a fragrant soup of connections
passing the bowl from one to another to partake in the feast of
love and unity.
Floating without regard for telephone wires or wind farms my
mind glides to a day in my childhood.
The new two tone Oldsmobile rests at the end of the sidewalk.
Four o' clock flowers adorn the front of the house. Kobuck, our
dog, barks and pulls at his chain wanting his freedom.
I just want to learn to ride my new bike, the one father promised
me for surviving polio.
My father comes out the side door of our brick house to give me
a lesson.
I pedal while he holds the back of the seat.
I am about to get my balance when my wife wakes me to tell me
I need to get up, the furnace
isn't working.

BLACK AND WHITE

The black and white sign above the door read: CAFE.
Upon entering It was apparent things were unusual.
I sat in a booth, the seat covered in white vinyl, the table top all black.
I waited patiently observing the one waitress moving about.
She held a white tray about shoulder height.
I could hear noises behind the kitchen door.
I waited and waited, my right leg jiggling up and down in frustration.
Finally, she approached my table then handed me a laminated single sheet.
On the face it said MENU in bold white print contrasting the all-black page.
Somewhat off center was a white dot. I paused was puzzled then replied,
"I will take that".
She did not speak just took her black pen and made a dot on her white order pad and reached for the menu.
Time passed slowly. The only movement was the waitress dressed in her white uniform with black nurses shoes and white hose.
A large very plain looking clock ticked loudly each minute that passed.
Many ticks later my waitress approached my table, her tray held high.
Lowering the tray, she picked up the white plate and placed it before me.
A seed lay in the center of the plate—just a seed.
I looked up at her in amazement. " What am I to do with this?" I inquired.
She replied, "You are here to learn patience.
Take it home and plant it. It will yield food if you care for it properly."

RIVER OF LIFE

Many times have I come to the edge of this roaring river,
reluctant to cross yet knowing opportunity, and growth lie on the
distant shore.
I find myself fearful of the potential consequences of attempting
the journey.
I ask myself if fear will keep me from growth, from change
or will I face the challenge and traverse the rapid waters?
I pause, pray, like I always do. The waters do not part for me
as they did for the Israelites escaping Egypt. The rapids could
take me to unwanted places or pull me under, ending my days.
Double minded, I squirm for a decision.
One mind warning to stay away, play it safe.
The other pulling at my conscious body, with me.
"Come with me, come.
Enter the challenge, don't let fear limit your life."
My history has been to cross, always finding growth on the other
shore.
Now, an older man, caution speaks louder,
"Don't risk it."
Faith and courage move my feet into the water.
I plunge in yet another time knowing the risk.
I must continue to swim through challenges to grow.

COVID ISOLATION

Today a fly entered the house through an open door.
Usually my instinct is to swat any fly near me but this felt
different.
I was alone, no dog or cat, bird or fish just me. My wife has been
away for a while.
I do have house plants but it alarms me when I find myself
talking to them.
I caught the fly by putting a clear plastic carry out container over
it while it walked on a window, lamenting its lost outdoor
freedom. Carefully,
I slid a piece of paper under the container, trapping the fly inside.
A few holes in the top allowed it to breathe while it quarantined.
A few days later after I allowed it to freely participate in my
home life.
Of course, there was just one fly so breeding masses of them
was unlikely.
Being confined to the house much more than usual, It was good
to have a friend.
Feeling sorry for it I trapped it again, took it in the bathroom, put
the container up to the mirror.
It soon began walking around, seemingly finding great joy with
its new found mate.
They spent a good amount of time on top of one another.
Time passed and the fly that I now refer to as "Bugs" began to
feel safe around me.
It often lands, casually walks around tickling the hairs on my arm
while we watch a Netflix documentary "about insects taking
over the world".
Even though it has been isolated from the outside world now for
many days,
I object when it lands on my sandwich looks up at me as if to ask
if the bread is organic.
I'm sorry to say today while leaving the house to pick up my wife

from the airport, "Bugs" left me.
I was so pleased to have my wife back, it made it easier to
accept my friend abandoning me.
I shared some stories with my wife about "Bugs" and my
relationship.
She was not jealous.
The next morning while peering out the large glass window,
near the kitchen table, I noticed a fly on the outside looking in.
I went close to the window to see if perhaps it was "Bugs".
I was not sure until he winked at me.
Without words I knew he returned to remind
me of those around the world that are alone
during this time without even a fly as a companion.

DRIVE THROUGH

Sunshine illuminated the glittery lavender paint job.
After cleaning this beauty I went to find my father.
He would occasionally let me drive his new '59 Cadillac
if I washed it. It was one with the large swept back tail fins
that would maim you if you bumped into them.
This particular Sunday afternoon a girl I was smitten about
would be working as a car hop at the local drive-in.
Permission was given to drive the car. I changed into what
I imagined to be my coolest clothes, played critically with my
hair, then drove off.
As I was nearing the drive- in, I steered over to the curb,
put the car in neutral, and began pulling levers and pushing
buttonsin an attempt to put down the convertible top.
Once the top had neatly folded itself properly away I continued
on.
But something felt odd. The slightest bump in the road
felt as if I was bouncing on a trampoline.
I was quite concerned about what I had done to the car,
but I was close enough to the drive-in to turn my focus on
how I would act when Judy walked up to the to take my order.
Should I be just real nice or should I act aloof or distracted?
The drive- in was a place where high school kids hung out.
They parked their cars all around the building.
A car hop would come to take your order.
I circled the building slowly hoping I would get Judy's attention.
A spot opened. I pull in and parked.
There were several car hops moving about but I did not see Judy.
I waited, trying to be patient. After a short while I thought
I would get out of the car and walk inside to make sure she was
working.
Reaching for the handle I pulled it to release the door latch.
Judy rounded the corner just as I stepped out of the car and fell
to the ground.

I lay there, her standing above me with a look: "What are you
doing down there expression"
on her face accompanied by a smirky smile.
While pulling or pushing levers to get the top to go down,
I ignited air bags that lifted the car up.
It was, for me, an unknown feature of the car,
created in case the huge trunk was loaded
and the car was full of passengers
so you could drive up an incline without dragging the pavement.
When I stepped from the car, I did not realize the air bags
had raised it up an extra 6 inches, causing my fall.
All my preparations to impress her were foiled.
I intended to ask her out, but this event left me convinced
this was the wrong time for that.

ENRICO

Enrico is a small man. Even if he was not so bowlegged he would
still be small.
Age has worn his hip bones causing his gait to be very deliberate
and slow.
He wears a brimmed hat with stains blotched here and there that
shades his aging, wrinkled face.
HIs home is meager located just outside this small beach village.
It is constructed from a variety of materials like tin, wood and
plastic.
It is a house unfit for living in a country not close to the equator.
Daily I have seen him passing through the quaint hotel where we
are staying.
Ever since my wife gave him a change purse full of coins
in his little woven basket he calls us both by my wife's name,
"Hola Bobbie," then shakes my hand. His right hand seems
unable to fully open, making his hand shake awkwardly but
sincere.
He is quite versatile. He plays the guitar and sings Spanish songs
around the village in the evenings. Afternoons he can be found
sitting on a corner stoop of the village center where he sells a
tasty ceviche out of a styrofoam cooler.
The ceviche is served in small plastic cups.
This evening I witnessed him and his unique walking style
making it along the road with guitar in hand with his long black
socks pulled up near his knees, wearing his Bob Marley over-
sized tee-shirt.
No doubt he is on his way to preform at local restaurants if
allowed.
After dinner my wife and I strolled though the streets to find our
way to the organic restaurant where it is open mic night.
To our surprise our Enrico was on stage singing and playing
guitar, his little straw basket soliciting some coins near his feet.
We made our way in to listen to him.

The crowd, mostly younger than us, chatted, paying little
attention while waiting for their type music to arrive as Enrico
sang his heart out.
I wanted to yell out and tell them to respect him,
but my voice would have fallen on deaf ears.
Have to give a lot of credit to him
for making his way in what can be a harsh world.

INFECTIOUS LAUGHTER

The sound of her laughter carried through the dense forest,
pierced the pane glass windows,
filling the room, the kind of laugh that, without knowing its
origin, infects you with joy.
Soon you are there laughing along with her and wondering why?
I went out on the veranda to see if I could spot the owner of that
voice.
Below, three teens were playing in the fresh water flowing from
the hills above the ocean.
Too far from hearing their subdued communication, I watched
them play.
Depending on the time of day the fresh water flows from above
out to the inviting ocean.
At high tide the ocean waves crash into the rendering fresh
water.
It is a place I am familiar with after many visits of staying in the
small, quaint hotel where people like myself come from various
parts of the world to vacation.
A place where the ocean flirts with the beach. Where plants
grow thick and generous.
Where animals have dense forests to forage and hunt in, to breed
in, to survive in.
It is a place where the full moon appears to rise from the ocean,
lays across its surface a trail of sparkling diamond atop the
water, giving the impression you could walk across them to the
surface of the moon.

NIGHT MOVES

Sitting cross legged on the damp blades, my slightly curved spine
leans me forward.
I close my eyes, listen. Insects vibrate to their own rhythm,
together creating an orchestra of sound.
In the distance falling water sets the melody.I realize I have a
visitor.
It lands, punctures my skin to withdraw from within the liquid
nourishment of its life.
I want to swat it but stop to feel, just experience. Gone now, after
the banquet,
I'm left with the impulse to scratch. I hold back, accepting my
fate.
I focus my full attention to the spot where it inserted its siphon
to feel the rise of my skin, to feel the stinging, itching reaction of
my winged intruder.
The deep darkness is slowly invaded as the glow of the evening
moon breaks above the dense trees.
Moment to moment, perpetually rising, it creates soft shadows.
Creatures once protected by the darkness now can see movement.
There is a sensation of danger among them. I sense their caution,
their acute awareness as they tip toe through the brush slowly,
scanning about them.
Suddenly, I have the feeling I am standing above myself
observing.
Perspective floats gently higher and higher until I see myself
sitting cross-legged on the cool damp blades from far above.
The further I go, the smaller I appear.
Now a tiny spot barely visible, I realize I am a minute part of it
all.
Moments ago it was all about me.
Now, part of the entire, I feel at one with the whole.

LIMITS…

I carry bugs out of the house rather than smashing them.
I am aware they are trying to survive, as I am.
If I see someone in distress I will do my best to help them.
It bothers me to dig in the garden and find I have dissected a
worm or grub.
I choose plants to add to my garden's beauty, plants that attract
bees and butterflies.
I provide a pond in which koi fish exist, toads come to mate.
Many creatures drink both winter and summer.
I feed birds and no longer cuss at squirrels' mischievous behavior,
Even at the cost of young plants being dug up by them or their
raiding of the bird feeders.
While driving I will do all I can to avoid squirrels while they do
their indecisive dance in the road.
I do volunteer work in order to help people in need.
I pray for world peace each day as well as for guidance in my
own seeking.
Yet… I have my limits, I am afraid.
An ant or two may be strolling around my sink seeking water
or tiny scraps to drag home to their families. It would be effort-
less to squash them leaving nothing more than a tiny spot. I
deliberately let them go about their way unless or until they are
joined by the members of their tribe forming a highway from nest
to sink. That is when they have to be confronted.
Attack is the mode necessary to stop the invasion. It disturbs me
greatly to don my armor, transforming my peaceful demeanor into
one of killing confrontation.
I grit my teeth, ask for forgiveness, then destroy.
Dogs bark. It is their nature to warn of potential danger.
My neighbor's dog is cute and nice. I like him but he tends to
bark at many things, too many things, until I want to hurt him or
find a way to have him arrested for disturbing the peace.
Two doves, the symbol of peace, coo to one another over and

over, over and over until I want to throw rocks at them to get
them to leave.
Can one sit and be bitten by mosquitoes and not react in violence?
It is my nature to seek compassion, to want peace. To desire love
in all actions and thoughts.
Is it also my nature to break down, to transform, to roll out the
tanks when I feel I am being overrun, when repetition takes me to
a place where my limits run out and I express violence?
Who wins that war wrestling within themselves? Where are the
lines drawn?
Individuals and nations seem to carry the same burden. How can I
hope for peace on earth when even within me there is a battle
sitting dormant waiting to be pushed to the edge?
Will I, will nations ever be capable of drawing the line
so far in the distance that peace, real peace is possible?
God has sent us a model, has sent us a man to walk the earth as
you and I do, who, like you and I, had to confront the dichotomy
each of us face each day.
We will never know if Jesus killed mosquitoes or grew angry at
incessant barking dogs.
What we do know that on the larger scale, He fully expressed a
way to bring peace to this earth.

THANK YOU HEAD

Entering the bathroom before me in the mirror,
I observed my head perched on my shoulders
looking out at my reflection. The head that has been carried
by my lower body all my days.
I look closely at it in a way I typically don't.
When I shave, brush my hair, I observe it,
but in a different way than this time.
Looking into the eyes I think of what they have done for me,
allowing me to view a gorgeous sunset displaying amazing
colors.
The blue sky, the fire red leaves that a burning bush wears in
autumn.
The range of colorful birds offered to my delight.
The beauty of my wife opening, like a flower in the early
morning.
My nose, standing out there, the first to arrive where ever I go.
It gifts me with the scent of a rose, a toasted cinnamon roll,
the tantalizing aroma of freshly brewed coffee.
My mouth surrounded by lips that touch another's, expressing
love.
They part when it is time to smile.
It allows me to taste the succulent spices of an Indian dinner,
the sweetness of a ripe peach, or the tang of red wine as it
tickles my tongue.
Those odd radar receptors we call ears. Holes that sound enters
allowing me to hear, a distant train whistle, a song that makes me
want to dance,
the sweet whisper of " I love you".
Thank you head.

TRANSFORMATION

My mother was a seeker of goodness. My father a collector/seller
of ancient manuscripts.
Having passed away suddenly a few months back they left me
buried in grief and unattended affairs.
At the advice of a good friend, I decided the way to seek clarity
and direction was to travel to the Amazon.
I was told that shaman use plant medicines ceremonies to induce
insight into trauma and release visions of the future.
Having arrived deep in the jungles of Peru, I found myself
trodding through muddy trails that eventually lead to the Shibibo
tribe village.
Fortunately, the first person I attempted to communicate with
knew a bit of English. She explained there were four other
foreigners currently attending the ceremony.
I was assigned a tiny cabin where I could live for the next week.
A knock at the door brought me face to face with a man from
America.
I enthusiastically invited him in.
He was on his fifth day in camp. He explained morning
gatherings were about purging, a cleansing in preparation
for an Ayhawaska ceremony. You will drink warm salt water until
you vomit.
This was the beginning of the cleansing process.
That will be followed by drinking various plant medicines
custom-designed to begin healing the physical ailments
you shared with the shaman at your interview.
That night, at my first ceremony, I sat before the shaman
in the light of a small candle that illuminated the wisdom in his
eyes.
I drank a one ounce shot glass amount of the plant brew,
threw it down like they do in the old Westerns.
It had an awful taste, making it very difficult to swallow.
The waiting began.

Near total darkness accentuated the intense jungle sounds.
Creatures and insects each expressing themselves created a
natural jungle orchestra.
Intricate colorful patterns began floating past my closed eyes.
Soon a carousel appeared with small train cars instead of horses.
I boarded one in hopes it would transport me to the town of
insight.
Turning the corner the car slipped into a golden curtain.
Before me stood a light green panda bear. Its eye balls were
rolling over like a slot machine, pausing now and then. They
stopped on dual images.
The panda would speak a message. I received one:
"Don't ever think you are alone in having deplorable thoughts
now and then.
Everyone has them. Only you can release yourself from their
effects.
Confront them with your mother's goodness.
They will dissolve into puddles of conscious growth."
The panda morphed into a dusty, worn book. it lay before me on a
delicately carved table the color of rust. I opened it.
The text was in a language foreign to me.
I looked around, not far from me was an old man sitting cross-
legged on top of a large toad stool. I approached him and inquired
if he knew the language within the old book.
Upon reaching for it, I noticed he was wearing a ring.
The unique ring looked just like the one my father
was given in trade for an ancient document.
My father told me it had special powers. He never told me what
they were.
I asked the man if his had anything unusual about it?
He replied it made him capable of translating any text written
throughout history.
He told me to have a seat. Instantly, a colorful folding chair
flipped open just behind me. I sat for a while, then became quite

anxious, my leg bouncing to the beat of the song "White Rabbit"
going on in my mind.
He looked up from the book, stared at me momentarily. He said it
speaks of a holy spirit that has existed before the sun, the planets,
the Universe.
before all matter. " He turned the page revealing what you have
come here for.
" Can you read it to me, I asked ?" " No, it is for you to ingest on
your own.
Hold the book, close your eyes and you will receive the
knowledge.
He handed me the book. I did as he said. My father's image
appeared before me.
He spoke, "Son, you already have the insight and wisdom you
need to become fully you.
That is all each of us can achieve. Trust yourself, know you have
within you the keys to your ultimate fulfillment. Cast out doubt
and uncertainty.
Your leadings lie within. Follow your instincts, they know your
path."
My father's presence floated off like a loose balloon on a windy
day.
My mother's hand appeared beckoning me to give her the book.
I knew it was her hand as she had passed on to me a unique
formation on my thumb like hers.
She reached out her other hand. I took it in mine.
The moment I took her hand in mine I returned to the ceremony.
Opening my eyes, I found the shaman sitting in front of me.
The bright moonlight allowed me to see his gesture for me to sit
up.
Placing his hands on my head, he began chanting,
guiding me back to present time and space.
The days passed quickly. The ceremony experiences each taught
me deep insights about life, happiness and forgiveness.

I left the Amazon having fulfilled my quest for healing past trauma as well having clarity in making future decisions on dealing with the unattended affairs my parents had left for me.

MEMORIES

Walking through a local park I found myself near
a softball field I played on many times over many years.
Tugged by history I approached the ball field.
A freshly laid infield surface awaits a new season.
Standing at the chain link fence near first base my fingers
gripped the still chilly metal,
I peered through the openings,
my mind drifted off like the smoke from the
chimney near by.
I could hear the sounds of past games,
the crack of the ball coming off the bat, the slap of the ball
landing in my leather mitt.
I could smell the freshly cut grass in the outfield,
where I found my home.
Ghosts of past teammates faces,
the winning hugs,
high fives
The National traveling team
I played on
The long bus rides,
anticipating the coming tournament.
The fun of horsing around with the guys along the way.
Our team winning second place in the entire country.
The emotional feeling when the plaque that read,
all Tournament team was handed to me.
So much history.
A few tears traveling down my cheeks brought me back
to the moment.
As I walked from the field I glanced back on occasion to
Bathe in a sweet reminder of past memories